D1882824

FEEDING THE MIND

FEEDING THE MIND

BY
LEWIS CARROLL

WITH A PREFATORY NOTE BY

WILLIAM H. DRAPER

KALPAZ

©Reserved

All rights reserved. No part of this work may be reproduced, stored, adapted, or transmitted in any form or by any means, electronic, mechanical, photocopying, micro-filming recording or otherwise, or translated in any language, without the prior written permission of the copyright owner and the publisher. The book is sold subject to the condition that it shall not, by way of trade or otherwise, be lent, resold, hired out, or otherwise circulated without the prior publisher's written consent in any form of binding or cover other than that in which it is published.

The views and opinions expressed in this book are author(s) own and the facts reported by them have been verified to the extent possible, and the publishers are not in any way liable for the same.

ISBN: 978-93-5128-707-0(HB)

First Published in 1907
Indian Reprint in 2017

Published by

Kalpaz Publications
C-30, Satyawati Nagar,
Delhi – 110052
E-mail: kalpaz@hotmail.com
Website: kalpazpublications.com
Ph.: +91-9212142040

NOTE

THE *history of this little sparkle from the pen of Lewis Carroll may soon be told. It was in October of the year* 1884 *that he came on a visit to a certain vicarage in Derbyshire, where he had promised, on the score of friendship, to do what was for him a most unusual favour—to give a lecture before a public audience.*

The writer well remembers his nervous, highly-strung manner as he stood before the little room full of simple people, few of whom had any idea of the world-wide reputation of that shy, slight figure before them.

NOTE

When the lecture was over, he handed the manuscript to me, saying: 'Do what you like with it.'

The one for whose sake he did this kindness was not long after called

'Into the Silent Land.'

So the beautifully-written MS., in his customary violet ink, has been treasured for more than twenty years, only now and then being read over at Christmas-time to a friend or two by the study fire, always to meet with the same welcome and glad acknowledgment that here was a genuine, though little flame that could not have belonged to any other source but that which all the world knew in Alice in Wonderland *and* Through the Looking-Glass.

There may be, perhaps, many others who, gathering round a winter fire, will be glad to read words, however few, from that bright source, and whose memories will respond to the fresh touch of that cherished name.

It remains to add but one or two more associations that cling to it and make the remembrance more vivid still. While Lewis Carroll was staying in the house, there came to call a certain genial and by no means shy Dean, who, without realizing what he was doing, proceeded, in the presence of other callers, to make some remark identifying Mr. Dodgson as the author of his books.

There followed an immense explosion immediately on the visitor's departure, with a pathetic and serious request that, if there were any risk of a repetition of the call, due warning might be given, and the retreat secured.

NOTE

Probably not many readers of the immortal Alice have ever seen the curious little whimsical paper called

EIGHT OR NINE WISE WORDS

ABOUT

LETTER-WRITING

which their author had printed and used to send to his acquaintance, accompanied by a small case for postage-stamps.

It consists of forty pages, and is published by Emberlin and Son, Oxford; and these are the contents:

In this little script, also, there are the same sparkles of wit which betoken that nimble pen, as, for example, under 'How to begin a Letter':

'"And never, never, dear madam" (N.B.—This remark is addressed to ladies *only*. No *man* would ever do such a thing), "put 'Wednesday' simply as the date! "*That way madness lies!*"'

From section 3: 'How to go on with a Letter.'—'A great deal of the bad writing in the world comes simply from writing too *quickly*. Of course you reply, "I do it to save *time*." A very good object, no doubt, but what right have you to do it at your friend's expense? Isn't *his* time as valuable as yours? Years ago I used to receive letters from a friend—and very interesting letters too—written in one of the most atrocious hands ever invented. It generally took me about a *week* to read one of his letters! I used to carry it about in my pocket and take it out at leisure times, to puzzle over the riddles which composed it—holding it in different positions and at different distances, till at last the meaning of some hopeless scrawl would flash upon me, when I at once wrote down the English under it. And when several had been thus guessed the context would help one with the others, till at last the whole series of hieroglyphics was deciphered. If *all* one's friends wrote like that, life would be entirely spent in reading their letters!'

Rule for correspondence that has, unfortunately, become controversial.

'*Don't repeat yourself.* — When once you have had your say fully and clearly on a certain point, and have failed to convince your friend, *drop that subject.* To repeat your arguments all over again, will simply lead to his doing the same, and so you will go on like a circulating decimal. *Did you ever know a circulating decimal come to an end?*'

Rule 5.—'If your friend makes a severe remark, either leave it unnoticed, or make your reply distinctly less severe; and if he makes a friendly remark, tending towards making up the little difference that has arisen between you, let your reply be distinctly *more* friendly.

'If, in picking a quarrel, each party declined to go more than *three-eighths* of the way, and if in making friends, each was ready to go *five-eighths* of the way—why, there would be more reconciliations than quarrels! Which is like the Irishman's remonstrance to his gad-about daughter: "Shure, you're *always* goin' out! You go out three times for *wanst* that you come in!"'

Rule 6.—'Don't try to get the last word. . . . (N.B.—If you are a gentleman and your friend a lady, this rule is superfluous: *You won't get the last word!*)'

Let the last word to-day be part of another rule, which gives a glimpse into that gentle heart:

'When you have written a letter that you feel may possibly irritate your friend, however necessary you may have felt it to so express yourself, *put it aside till the next day.* Then read it over again, and fancy it addressed to yourself. This will often lead to your writing it all over again, taking out a lot of the vinegar and pepper and putting in honey instead, and thus making a *much* more palatable dish of it!'

> 'Quis desiderio sit pudor aut modus
> Tam cari capitis?'

W. H. D.

November 1907.

FEEDING THE MIND

BREAKFAST, dinner, tea; in extreme cases, breakfast, luncheon, dinner, tea, supper, and a glass of something hot at bedtime. What care we take about feeding the lucky body! Which of us does as much for his mind? And what causes the difference? Is the body so much the more important of the two?

By no means: but life depends on the body being fed, whereas we can continue to exist as animals (scarcely as men) though the mind be utterly starved and neglected. Therefore Nature provides that, in case of serious neglect of the body, such terrible consequences of discomfort and pain shall ensue, as will soon bring us back to a sense of our duty: and some of the functions necessary to life she does for us altogether, leaving us no choice in the matter. It would fare but ill with many of us if we were left to superintend our own digestion and circulation. 'Bless me!' one would cry, 'I forgot to wind up my heart this morning! To think that it has been standing still for the last three hours!' 'I can't walk with you this afternoon,' a friend would say, 'as I have no less than eleven dinners to digest. I had to let them stand over from last week, being so busy, and my doctor says he will not answer for the consequences if I wait any longer!'

Well, it is, I say, for us that the consequences of neglecting the body can be clearly seen and felt; and it might be well for some if the mind were equally visible and tangible—if we could take it, say, to the doctor, and have its pulse felt.

'Why, what have you been doing with this mind lately? How have you fed it? It looks pale, and the pulse is very slow.'

'Well, doctor, it has not had much regular food lately. I gave it a lot of sugar-plums yesterday.'

'Sugar-plums! What kind?'

'Well, they were a parcel of conundrums, sir.'

'Ah, I thought so. Now just mind this: if you go on playing tricks like that, you'll spoil all its teeth, and get laid up with mental indigestion. You must have nothing but the plainest reading for the next few days. Take care now! No novels on any account!'

Considering the amount of painful experience many of us have had in feeding and dosing the body, it would, I think, be quite worth our while to try and translate some of the rules into corresponding ones for the mind.

First, then, we should set ourselves

to provide for our mind its *proper kind* of food. We very soon learn what will, and what will not, agree with the body, and find little difficulty in refusing a piece of the tempting pudding or pie which is associated in our memory with that terrible attack of indigestion, and whose very name irresistibly recalls rhubarb and magnesia; but it takes a great many lessons to convince us how indigestible some of our favourite lines of reading are, and again and again we make a meal of the unwholesome novel, sure to be followed by its usual train of low spirits, unwillingness to work, weariness of existence—in fact, by mental nightmare.

Then we should be careful to provide this wholesome food in *proper amount*. Mental gluttony, or over-reading, is a dangerous propensity, tending to weakness of digestive power, and in some cases to loss of appetite: we know that bread is a good and wholesome food, but who would like to try the experiment of eating two or three loaves at a sitting?

I have heard a physician telling his patient—whose complaint was merely gluttony and want of exercise—that 'the earliest symptom of hyper-nutrition is a deposition of adipose tissue,' and no doubt the fine long words greatly consoled the poor man under his increasing load of fat.

I wonder if there is such a thing in nature as a FAT MIND? I really think I have met with one or two: minds which could not keep up with the slowest trot in conversation; could not jump over a logical fence, to save their lives; always got stuck fast in a narrow argument; and, in short, were fit for nothing but to waddle helplessly through the world.

Then, again, though the food be wholesome and in proper amount, we know that we must not consume *too many kinds at once.* Take the thirsty a quart of beer, or a quart of cider, or even a quart of cold tea, and he will probably thank you (though not so heartily in the last case!). But what think you his feelings would be if you offered him a tray containing a little mug of beer, a little mug of cider, another of cold tea, one of hot tea, one of coffee, one of cocoa, and corresponding vessels of milk, water, brandy-and-water, and butter-milk? The sum total might be a quart, but would it be the same thing to the haymaker?

Having settled the proper kind, amount, and variety of our mental food, it remains that we should be careful to allow *proper intervals* between meal and meal, and not swallow the food hastily without mastication, so that it may be thoroughly digested; both which rules, for the body, are also applicable at once to the mind.

First, as to the intervals: these are as really necessary as they are for the body, with this difference only, that while the body requires three or four hours' rest before it is ready for another meal, the mind will in many cases do with three or four minutes. I believe that the interval required is much shorter than is generally supposed, and from personal experience, I would recommend anyone, who has to devote several hours together to one subject of thought, to try the effect of such a break, say once an hour, leaving off for five minutes only each time, but taking care to throw the mind absolutely 'out of gear' for those five minutes, and to turn it entirely to other subjects. It is astonishing what an amount of impetus and elasticity the mind recovers during those short periods of rest.

And then, as to the mastication of the food, the mental process answering to this is simply *thinking over* what we read. This is a very much greater exertion of mind than the mere passive taking in the contents of our Author. So much greater an exertion is it, that, as Coleridge says, the mind often 'angrily refuses' to put itself to such trouble—so much greater, that we are far too apt to neglect it altogether, and go on pouring in fresh food on the top of the undigested masses already lying there, till the unfortunate mind is fairly swamped under the flood. But the greater the exertion the more valuable, we may be sure, is the effect. One hour of steady thinking over a subject (a solitary walk is as good an opportunity for the process as any other) is worth two or three of reading only. And just consider another effect of this thorough digestion of the books we read; I mean the arranging and 'ticketing,' so to speak, of the subjects in our minds, so that we can readily refer to them when we want them. Sam Slick tells us that he has learnt several languages in his life, but somehow 'couldn't keep the parcels sorted' in his mind. And many a mind that hurries through book after book, without waiting to digest or arrange anything, gets into that sort of condition, and the unfortunate owner finds himself far from fit really to support the character all his friends give him.

'A thoroughly well-read man. Just you try him in any subject, now. You can't puzzle him.'

You turn to the thoroughly well-read man. You ask him a question, say, in English history (he is understood to have just finished reading Macaulay). He smiles good-naturedly, tries to look as if he knew all about it, and proceeds to dive into his mind for the answer. Up comes a handful of very promising facts, but on examination they turn out to belong to the wrong century, and are pitched in again. A second haul brings up a fact much more like the real thing, but, unfortunately, along with it comes a tangle of other things—a fact in political economy, a rule in arithmetic, the ages of his brother's children, and a stanza of Gray's 'Elegy,' and among all these, the fact he wants has got hopelessly twisted up and entangled. Meanwhile, every one is waiting for his reply, and, as the silence is getting more and more awkward, our well-read friend has to stammer out some half-answer at last, not nearly so clear or so satisfactory as an ordinary schoolboy would have given. And all this for want of making up his knowledge into proper bundles and ticketing them.

Do you know the unfortunate victim of ill-judged mental feeding when you see him? Can you doubt him? Look at him drearily wandering round a reading-room, tasting dish after dish—we beg his pardon, book after book—keeping to none. First a mouthful of novel; but no, faugh! he has had nothing but that to eat for the last week, and is quite tired of the taste. Then a slice of science; but you know at once what the result of that will be—ah, of course, much too tough for *his* teeth. And so on through the whole weary round, which he tried (and failed in) yesterday, and will probably try and fail in to-morrow.

Mr. Oliver Wendell Holmes, in his very amusing book, 'The Professor at the Breakfast Table,' gives the following rule for knowing whether a human being is young or old: 'The crucial experiment is this—offer a bulky bun to the suspected individual just ten minutes before dinner. If this is easily accepted and devoured, the fact of youth is established.' He tells us that a human being, 'if young, will eat anything at any hour of the day or night.'

To ascertain the healthiness of the *mental* appetite of a human animal, place in its hands a short, well-written, but not exciting treatise on some popular subject—a mental *bun*, in fact. If it is read with eager interest and perfect attention, *and if the reader can answer questions on the subject afterwards*, the mind is in first-rate working order. If it be politely laid down again, or perhaps lounged over for a few minutes, and then, 'I can't read this stupid book! Would you hand me the second volume of "The Mysterious Murder"?' you may be equally sure that there is something wrong in the mental digestion.

If this paper has given you any useful hints on the important subject of reading, and made you see that it is one's duty no less than one's interest to 'read, mark, learn, and inwardly digest' the good books that fall in your way, its purpose will be fulfilled.